TACKLING THE TABOO

Navigating Anxiety, Depression, and Other Mental Illnesses as a Christian

Terica Turner

MindWell
Birmingham, AL

MindWell
Birmingham, Alabama

Edited by: Teresa Crumpton

ISBN: 979-8-9954961-0-6

DEDICATION

I dedicate this book, with love, to my late, sweet, loving, kind-hearted Granny, Mrs. Annie Grace Turner.

ACKNOWLEDGMENTS

So many people have helped me while on my journey to wellness, in so many different ways. Many thanks to Dr. B, Dr. S, Nurse Alanda, and my entire team of mental health professionals who've helped me get to a point of stability. To Malika, thank you for going with me to that very first counseling appointment and recommending my team of professionals. Your support means everything. To my dear sister and my brother in Christ, Frizzette, and Carwaskie, you helped me more than you'll ever know. I love and appreciate you and couldn't ask to know better people. To Tim and Donna, your kindness towards me means more than I can say – thank you. To Dewana, thank you for being my sister-friend – always a great listener, never judgmental. To Cindy, thanks for helping me gain a piece of serenity when everything around me was chaos. And thanks for encouraging me to write – and to write this book. Jania, thank you for the example you always are to me. Thank you for proofing those very first drafts of my manuscript. And thank you for being there for me when I need you the most. Lastly, thanks to my family and all those who show love for and care towards me. I thank God for you and the role that each of you has played in helping me to overcome the challenges related to my mental illnesses. Without all of you, I don't know where I'd be.

TABLE OF CONTENTS

INTRODUCTION

When he came to my door to take me away, I had no idea my family had gone behind my back and filed a petition with the court to have me legally committed. Even my psychiatrist was in on the ambush! And no one warned me, helped me understand, or got me ready.

Thankfully, when the sheriff came knocking, I had just left the house, and I only knew about it because my concerned brother-in-law called me on the phone. He told me about what had nearly happened at the hands of my scheming sisters.

Can you imagine that? Me—a Christ-abiding, law-fearing citizen—in handcuffs! Well, maybe no handcuffs, but still, it was unthinkable.

I do not even know where the sheriff would have taken me—to a hospital, a mental-health asylum, or the courthouse. But wherever he would have taken me, I didn't want to be there. Writing and thinking about it now, several years later, it still upsets me.

I am still not sure why my family felt they had to go to that extreme. There was no need to go that route. I mean, looking back, I know I was having some serious mental health issues, but I do not think I needed to be committed to a hospital or anywhere else. And I was working hard at getting well. I was seeing a counselor and had even made improvements. If only they had sat with me and discussed the issue, we could have avoided all the turmoil their actions caused. I literally could not go home because I did not know if someone would show up with a straight-jacket to forcibly take me away. I could not go to my family members' houses because I did not know who was in on the so-called intervention. I had nowhere to go. And I felt that I did not have a friend that I could trust. So, I fled the state with intention of never returning or speaking to my family again.

Sure, my family loved me – even though at the time I could not see how – but they did not know how to deal with a family member struggling with mental illness. They did not know how to talk to me, and they did not know what it was like to have a mental illness. It was as if the topic was off-limits. They did not know how much the ambush would hurt me. And they believed they had to work in the shadows to try and handle a situation that involved me, without me.

Unfortunately, for many families and individuals and among the faithful, mental illness is a taboo topic. People simply do not talk about it. They see issues in people close to them, and even in themselves, and they ignore them. Or they try to deal with the issues in inappropriate or unhealthy ways.

As a result, people who are already struggling get hurt. Millions of Americans experience mental illness and the struggles that go with it, and Christians are not exempt. Our sisters and brothers are struggling and suffering in silence. But it does not have to be that way.

This book is written to help create a dialogue about mental illness, how it affects Christians, and ways it can be helped. Because we love God and have faith does not mean we will not get sick mentally, just as it does not mean we will not get sick physically.

My hope is that this book will help you identify mental illnesses, recognize myths associated with them, and know the facts. Most of all, I hope you will better be able to love and serve one another through a better understanding of those afflicted with mental health issues (Romans 12:15).

It is important to note that this book is in no way a substitute for professional medical advice, counseling, treatment, or medication for mental illnesses. If you or someone you know is experiencing mental health issues, *please seek professional help*. And if you or someone you know is suicidal, in crisis, or in immediate danger, please call your local emergency numbers.

If my family had read this book, maybe they never would have tried to have me put away against my own will. Maybe they would have been able to discuss with me my struggles with mental illness, and they would not have caused a years-long rift between us.

I pray that no other person will have to experience what I went through with mental illness. That is why I draw upon my own experiences and the Bible to relay to you, the reader, the importance of taking mental health seriously. I hope that you will. Now let's tackle the taboo!

PART I:

BIBLICAL EXAMPLES OF MENTAL ILLNESS

"Be anxious for nothing, but in everything by prayer and supplication, with thanksgiving, let your requests be made known to God."

(Philippians 4:6)

1

ANXIETY IN THE HEART

My heart was pounding. I couldn't breathe. Everything around seemed to be closing in on me. Dark figures approached me down the aisle from a distance. I dropped the basket in my hands. As quickly as I could, I hurried out and rushed to my car. What was I thinking, going into a place like that, believing everything would be okay?

Once I got out of that grocery store, the panic attack subsided. (And thankfully, there had only been an empty basket in my hand when I dropped it!) The way I jetted out of there, you might think I had stumbled upon a crime scene in which I was the target. But it was only the neighborhood Winn-Dixie.

I look back now and wonder, "What was I thinking?!" But it was not uncommon for my anxiety to get the best of me when I ventured out into public places. Even a trip to the grocery store or worship services was difficult because I felt anxious about being around other people. And I'm not the only one.

"Approximately 18 percent of the population of the United States, or over 50 million people, have suffered from panic attacks, phobias, or other anxiety disorders in the past year."[1] That is a great number of people, especially since that does not include common kinds of anxiety or anxiousness. There is a difference between being worried about something and having an anxiety disorder. Similarly, there is a distinction between anxiety and fear.

Anxiety Disorders vs. Worry

Everyone worries from time to time and sometimes feels anxious about a job, relationship, or health. These are forms of common anxiety. Excessive worrying most of the time for more than six months constitutes an anxiety disorder. This type of anxiety interferes with normal functioning and activities of daily living. The umbrella of anxiety disorders covers panic disorders, agoraphobia (fear of being in public spaces), separation anxiety, and other phobias.

For a long time, I was afflicted with agoraphobia. I could not leave my house. I would try to go places but ended up turning around and heading back home. And if I managed to actually arrive at my destination, I would have a panic attack.

With proper treatment – counseling and medication – I was able to overcome my fear of being in public places. So, I know it's possible to make progress and improve your

---

[1] Bourne, Edmund J. *The Anxiety and Phobia Workbook.* Oakland: New Harbinger Publications, Inc., 2015, 1.

anxiety disorders or improve common anxiety in general. We are commanded not to be anxious (Philippians 4:6), so there must be a way for us to overcome our anxiety. God would not command us to do something that we are not able to accomplish (1 Corinthians 10:13). He will never put more on us than we can bear.

Anxious People in the Bible

Have you ever considered that God recorded for us examples of anxious people? Let's look at a few. Mary and Joseph anxiously sought for twelve-year-old Jesus while He was in the temple (Luke 2:48). King Nebuchadnezzar was so anxious about his dreams that he could not sleep before Daniel eventually interpreted them (Daniel 2:3). And Job was vexed in his soul because of the turmoil, loss, and physical maladies he faced (Job 27:2, KJV).

One example of an anxious person stands out, especially since Jesus Himself called her anxious. Remember Martha? She had welcomed Jesus into her home.

> *"And she had a sister called Mary, who also sat at Jesus' feet and heard His Word. But Martha was distracted with much serving, and she approached Him and exclaimed, "Lord, do You not care that my sister has left me to serve alone? Therefore, tell her to help me"* (Luke 10:39-40).

We have probably all been there when we have had guests in our homes. We want to make things nice and comfortable for our visitors. Sometimes, we are in the kitchen and hardly spend time with them because we are busy preparing. Well, Martha became very distracted and was worried about serving.

Jesus told her, *"Martha, Martha, you are worried and troubled about many things"* (Luke 10:41). The word for *worried* in the original Greek language is *merimnao.* According to *Strong's Concordance*, it means "to worry, to have anxiety, to be concerned." Martha had anxiety, and Jesus wanted to emphasize to her that she was anxious and didn't need to be. Notice that Jesus called Martha's name twice. Whenever the Lord wanted to emphasize what He was about to say, He called the name of the person to whom He was talking two times. Remember on the road to Damascus, the Lord called out, *"Saul, Saul, why are you persecuting Me?"* (Acts 9:4). When God called Samuel, He also called his name twice (1 Samuel 3:10). He did the same with Moses (Exodus 3:4). In those instances, the Lord wanted to emphasize His desire for the person whom He was calling to follow Him.

When God called a person's name twice, He meant business. He wanted Saul to be instrumental in growing the church. He wanted Samuel to be a prophet. And He wanted Moses to lead His people.

In this case, the Lord wanted Martha to stop being anxious, sit at His feet, and listen to His Word (Luke 10:42). Jesus was serious. He explained that Mary had chosen the good part, so obviously being anxious and worried was the bad part.

The Lord does not want us to have anxiety over anything. He desires that we seek Him and His kingdom first and let everything else fall into place. He said, *"Therefore do not worry about tomorrow, for tomorrow will worry about its own things. Sufficient for the day is its own trouble"* (Matthew 6:34). In the present, we have enough things to occupy our attention. We should not be worried about what is out of our control. We must be like Mary and choose the good part, which is hearing the Word of Christ.

We can be less anxious by changing our thinking. Romans 12:2 tells us to be transformed by the renewing of our minds. We must work diligently to renew our thinking. David prayed to God: *"Create in me a clean heart, O God, and renew a steadfast spirit within me"* (Psalm 51:10). "Steadfast" means fixed in the right direction, resolute, and unwavering. If we want to get rid of our anxieties, we have to be firm, resolute, and unwavering in our commitment to do so. And the way we renew our minds and change our thinking is by studying God's Word.

The Word says to be anxious for nothing but, instead, to meditate on things that are true, things that are noble, things that are just, things that are pure, things that are lovely, and things that are of good report (Philippians 4:8). Whatever we are anxious about, God can take care of it. We just have to take it to Him in prayer, giving thanks to Him as our Father.

Questions for Reflection

1. How did God capture Moses' attention at the burning bush?

2. Read Exodus 3:1-5:

    Now Moses was tending the flock of Jethro his father-in-law, the priest of Midian. And he led the flock to the back of the desert, and came to Horeb, the mountain of God. And the Angel of the Lord appeared to him in a flame of fire from the midst of a bush. So he looked, and behold, the bush was burning with fire, but the bush was not consumed. Then Moses said, "I will now turn aside and see this great sight, why the bush does not burn." So when the Lord saw that he turned aside to look, God called to him from the midst of the bush and said, "Moses, Moses!" Then He said, "Do not draw near this place. Take your sandals off your feet, for the place where you stand is holy ground."

    What did God tell Moses to do after He gained his attention?

3. Read Philippians 4:6-8. What will the peace of God do for you?

4. How can we transform our thinking each day? Give Scriptures to support your answer.

5. What are some things that make you anxious?

6. How do you manage your anxiety about those things?

7. Locate 1 Peter 5:7 and write the verse here. Let it be your memory verse for the week.

8. Read Genesis 46:1-7. Who else did God call by name twice?

9. What important message did He have to tell him/her?

"In my distress I called upon the Lord, and cried out to my God; He heard my voice from His temple, and my cry came before Him, even to His ears."

(Psalm 18:6)

2

DEPRESSION IN THE DEVOUT

We're human. We lose. We grieve. We grieve the loss of relationships, the loss of jobs, the loss of health, and the loss of life. To some degree, we have all been depressed at some point in our lives.

When I married a gospel preacher, I never expected that he would become an atheist. But, he did. I also never expected that we would get divorced. But, we did. And I went through a deep, dark depression. I did not eat much at all for months; I simply had no appetite. I barely made it to work. And, I cried more than I can remember at any other point in my life. I was severely depressed. At least I lost some unwanted weight. That is the one thing I miss about my depression. Those were the days (not really).

Seriously, though, according to the National Institute of Mental Health,

> *"depression (major depressive disorder or clinical depression) is a common but serious mood disorder. It causes severe symptoms that affect how you feel, think, and handle daily*

> *activities, such as sleeping, eating, or working."*[2]

Major depressive disorder is characterized by a period of two or more weeks of an individual having a depressed mood or loss of pleasure in activities of daily living, with symptoms including disturbance in sleeping, changes in eating, problems with energy, issues with concentration, or pervading thoughts of death.

A person can feel down and discouraged but not be experiencing a depressive episode. Symptoms must be persistently present to classify as depression. Some people may not even realize they are experiencing depression, but the signs are clear. When you are in a depression, it can be hard to see things for yourself. You may gradually stop eating or begin binging on junk foods (or whatever you can find) all the time. Or you might just think you are a smidge more tired than normal, so you sleep more. It may take a friend or family member to help a person recognize the state she is in and her need for help.

Hannah

While the Bible does not specifically identify anyone as "depressed," we do observe symptoms of depression in many people. Hannah showed signs of depression. She was barren and wanted to have children of her own. She was, in essence, being bullied by her husband's other wife,

---

[2] National Institute of Mental Health (2021). *Depression*. Retrieved May 4, 2022, from https://www.nimh.nih.gov/health/topics/depression.

Peninnah, because she had kids but Hannah did not. *"And her rival also provoked her severely, to make her miserable, because the Lord had closed her womb"* (1 Samuel 1:6). Hannah wept and did not eat anything (1 Samuel 1:7). *"And she was in bitterness of soul, and prayed to the Lord and wept in anguish"* (1 Samuel 1:10). Hannah was depressed; she had a "sorrowful spirit" (1 Samuel 1:15). But she prayed to the Lord, and He heard her petitions before Him. Our stations in life, or situations like Hannah's, can bring us down in our spirits. They can make us bitter in our souls.

The Hebrew word for bitterness in the text is *mar,* which is a form of *marah.* Based on Strong's concordance it means "bitter, bitterness, or bitterly, angry, chafed, discontented, great, or heavy."

Naomi

That brings Naomi to mind. Recall that Naomi lost her husband, and then her two sons died. She was left with only her two daughters-in-law: Ruth and Orpah. Orpah went back home to her family, but Ruth stayed with Naomi. When the two women went back to Naomi's home in Bethlehem, she told the women there, *"Do not call me Naomi, call me Mara, for the Almighty has dealt very bitterly with me"* (Ruth 1:20).

She was grieving the loss of her entire immediate family, so much so that she did not even want to be called by her name. She basically told them to call her bitter, discontented, heavy. She was heavy with grief and sadness, and understandably so. But she helped Ruth find her kinsman-redeemer, and the Lord blessed her with a grandchild (Ruth 4:13-17).

The Shunammite Woman

The Shunammite woman is another biblical case study on depression. Her only son died and the Bible says that her soul was in "deep distress" (2 Kings 4:27). She went to Elisha the prophet, knelt, and grabbed him by the feet. She was in such despair. The man of God heard her cry for help, and he prayed to the Lord. The Lord heard Elisha's prayer for the child and revived the boy (2 Kings 4:32-37).

Seeking Help

The three women mentioned above were depressed because of lack and loss. Hannah lacked children. Naomi lost her husband and her two sons. And the Shunammite woman lost her son. When we lose our relationships, our careers, or our health, we are bound to grieve and become depressed for some time. We may not want to continue our normal activities. We may eat significantly less or more. And we may lose the energy and concentration to be able to do much of anything. It is a natural response, but we should not let it keep on, unchecked, for long without making efforts to get ourselves out of the depression.

Notice that each of the women did not abide in their depression without seeking help. Hannah prayed to the Lord. Naomi helped someone else in need—her daughter-in-law Ruth. And the Shunammite woman sought the prophet Elisha who prayed for her son and revived him.

We must not sit idly and wallow in our depression. We can pray to the Lord. We can help someone else and, in turn, help ourselves feel better. And we can seek the help of professionals, who know what they are doing and who can help us.

The Scriptures provide examples of people being depressed and dealing with it appropriately. Often, we have to just find the right tools and resources to use so we can deal with depression, and we will discuss more of these as we progress through this study.

Questions for Reflection

1. How is having a "down-in-the-dumps-day" different from depression?

2. How can you recognize depression in yourself or someone else?

3. What symptoms of depression are easiest to spot?

4. Research the name Naomi using a lexicon. What is its meaning?

5. Read Exodus 15:22-25. Why did Naomi want to change her name to Mara?

6. Read 1 Samuel 1:10-18. What did Hannah do to make her face no longer sad?

7. How can prayer help us when we are feeling down?

8. Write out two verses to support your answer.

“Thus, my heart was grieved, and
I was vexed in my mind.”

(Psalm 73:21)

3

WARFARE IN THE MIND

It was a year or so after I fled my home state for fear of being locked away in a mental asylum. Sunday night after church services, I pulled out of the Home Depot's parking lot a happy camper. I had finally found a way to beat the intruders at their own game! When I arrived back at my third-floor apartment, I proceeded to board up my patio door with the eight planks of wood I had just bought. The boarded-up door would keep out those disrespectful people who had been breaking into my home every night while I was asleep. They would not get in without some very loud noise. That was sure to wake me. *That patio door must be where they'd been getting in.*

You see, every night I already secured the front door with a security bar, I had a security camera installed, and I had a monitored alarm system. And, so no one could enter my bedroom at night, I barricaded that interior door too.

But I just knew someone was still getting into my apartment and trying to hurt me. You would think that I would have felt safe in my bedroom behind all that security, but I ended up sleeping on the bedroom-closet floor. When the closet floor did not feel safe enough, I hauled my covers and pillow outside and slept in my car. And when the apartment's parking lot felt unsafe, I drove to the police station and tried to sleep in their parking lot. Once, even a church's parking lot made a safe place to sleep in my car.

But there I was, paying about $900 a month for rent and could not even sleep safely in my own home—or so I thought. Now, I realize that anything could have happened to me sleeping outside like that. My apartment was probably much safer.

But at that time, I simply did not feel safe at home. If someone had been breaking into my home, I would have caught it on the security tape videos that I watched and reviewed religiously when I came home from work—and sometimes before work. But that logic did not register in my mind. No matter what anyone told me, I could not be convinced that no one was breaking into my home - even with all the layers of security that I had put in place.

Schizophrenia

I was suffering from schizophrenia—a delusional disorder characterized by maintaining false opinions and beliefs that are fixed and unchangeable, even after being confronted with facts. Paranoia goes hand-in-hand with schizophrenia. So do racing thoughts, distrust and suspicion of others, difficulty sleeping or oversleeping, not leaving home, the belief that someone is spying on or stalking you, hearing voices, and the inability to sit for long periods of time.

Unfortunately, I can put a checkmark next to all those symptoms. To me, it seemed very possible that landlords or previous tenants would leave hidden cameras in bathrooms and in people's personal spaces. Maybe I should have never watched the movie *13 Cameras*. But for a long time, I thought people were spying on me and watching me without my consent. That belief nearly drove me insane. In my house, I covered the ceilings, walls, doors, televisions, and mirrors with anything that I could—sheets, duct tape, paper, and posters—because I believed there were hidden cameras in my home. Looking back, it all seems silly, and I can laugh at myself now. But at the time, it was very real and serious.

Still, as I write this, to me, nothing is ever what it seems to be. There is always some underlying motive to people's actions. On many occasions I have driven several miles out of my way because I was convinced someone was following me. In reality, I probably just wasted my gas. But that is the nature of the illness.

According to the National Alliance on Mental Illness, an estimated 1.5 million Americans have schizophrenia; about 7 million U.S. adults struggle with bipolar disorder; about 9 million people deal with post-traumatic stress disorder, and; an estimated 3.5 million adults in the U.S. experience borderline personality disorder.[3] In 2020 alone, 21 percent of adults in the U.S. experienced some form of mental

---

[3] National Alliance on Mental Illness. 2022. *Mental Health By The Numbers.* Accessed July 5, 2022. https://www.nami.org/Learn-More/Mental-Health-By-the-Numbers.

illness. That's about 1 in every 5 adults.[4] Many people are suffering, and we need to be aware. All mental illnesses can cause a significant change in one's ability to carry out normal activities of daily living.

Solomon said there is nothing new under the sun (Ecclesiastes 1:9), so people have been dealing with mental health issues since long ago. We can see several examples in the Bible.

Demon Possession and Mental Illness

Sometimes people mistakenly assume that individuals with mental illnesses (especially psychotic disorders) are demon-possessed. Remember the demon-possessed man from the Gospel of Mark? *"And always, night and day, he was in the mountains and in the tombs, crying out and cutting himself with stones"* (Mark 5:5). The man was engaging in behaviors indicative of mental illness. Cutting and other self-injurious behaviors are signs of serious mental health issues.

Let's be sure to make the distinction that demon possession is not equivalent to mental illness. If someone is mentally ill, he is not possessed by demons. People who were demon-possessed in the Bible were subject to mental illness, perhaps more so than someone who was not. While people who were possessed by demons often showed signs of physical or mental illness, the illnesses were quite distinct from the demon. The Bible makes clear that people

---

4 National Alliance on Mental Illness. 2022. *Mental Health By The Numbers.* Accessed July 5, 2022. https://www.nami.org/Learn-More/Mental-Health-By-the-Numbers.

who were sick and people who were demon-possessed were not one and the same. *"At evening, when the sun had set, they brought to Him all who were sick and those who were demon-possessed"* (Mark 1:32).

We need not assume that someone who is afflicted with schizophrenia, bipolar disorder, borderline personality disorder, or some other psychotic, mood, or personality disorder is possessed by demons. These are real illnesses that affect real people. Unlike demon possession, miracles are not required to overcome mental disorders.

David Pretends to be Mentally Ill

The Bible records the story of a man who many people thought was mentally ill. You may have heard of him. Bear-killing, lion-striking, giant-slaying, sheep-keeping, psalm-writing David. Yes, King David.

Well, technically, he was not king just yet. Saul was still reigning over the people of Israel as King. But David had been anointed to be the next king of Israel by the prophet Samuel (1 Samuel 16:1, 13). After that, when David killed Goliath—giant champion of the Philistine army—the women of Israel came out of the cities celebrating.

> *"So the women sang as they danced, and said: 'Saul has slain his thousands, And David his ten thousands.' Then Saul was very angry, and the saying displeased him; and he said, 'They have ascribed to David ten thousands, and to me they have ascribed only thousands. Now what more can he have but the kingdom?' So Saul*

> *eyed David from that day forward"* (1 Samuel 18:7-9).

After some time, King Saul not only resented David, but he tried to kill him. So, David had to flee for his life. He was on the run from Saul when he ended up in a place called Gath. David went to the king of Gath, Achish. When King Achish recognized him as the David the women had been singing about slaying ten thousands, David became afraid. So, he changed his behavior and acted like he was insane.

> *"Now David took these words to heart, and was very much afraid of Achish the king of Gath. So he changed his behavior before them, pretended madness in their hands, scratched on the doors of the gate, and let his saliva fall down on his beard. Then Achish said to his servants, "Look, you see the man is insane. Why have you brought him to me?"* (1 Samuel 21:12-14).

I do not know which particular mental illness David could have pretended to have; he just did not want Achish to kill him. But many people hold onto the notion that someone who is mentally ill has extremely chaotic behavior like David's. But that is not always the case.

Everyone who is mentally ill is not walking around with slobber all on their faces or scratching doors. Some may be boarding up doors, but not everyone does that. It is a misconception to believe that all mentally ill have extreme behaviors; just like the misconception that people who are mentally ill are demon-possessed.

But one thing I want to note is that David's behavior changed, and it made Achish *think* he was insane. That is the key to knowing when you or someone you love may be sick mentally—they exhibit a change in behavior.

When someone's behavior changes drastically, it is a tell-tale sign that something is wrong and they need help. The body acts on what the mind is thinking. As a man *"thinks in his heart, so is he"* (Proverbs 23:7). And out of the heart (or mind) flows the issues of life (Proverbs 4:23). So, if in my mind, I do not feel safe, then my actions will follow. Similarly, if a person thinks she is alone or that the weight of the world is on her shoulders with no help in sight, she will act accordingly. That's why we have to be careful to guard our hearts *and* minds.

For instance, I have no business watching movies like *13 Cameras*. The movie is about landlords and people leaving cameras in other people's homes and spying on them and even breaking-and-entering while they are away. I already have concerns about my safety, and I do not trust people that much, so watching a movie like that will only produce more anxiety, fear, and a sense of being unsafe. Entertainment choices are important. I have heard it said that if you let garbage come in, then garbage will come out.

And what works for one person who is mentally ill may not work for the next person. There is not a one-size-fits-all approach to dealing with mental health issues.

Recognizing Changes in Behavior

Mental illness can be managed through proper care and treatment. It is not something that should make us afraid of another person because he or she is afflicted with or affected by the illness. And when it comes to the spiritual realm, a person is not demon-possessed because they are mentally ill. Nor do people afflicted with mental illness always exhibit extreme behaviors. However, changes in behavior are key to help recognize when something is seriously wrong with you or someone you love.

Thankfully, there are tools and resources we can use to help manage these conditions and help people who struggle with them. We will discuss more of these solutions in later chapters. But first, we must discuss a topic that is off-limits for many people but needs serious consideration: suicide.

Questions for Reflection

1. Why do some people argue that demon possession in the Bible was merely a sickness or mental illness?

2. How can self-injurious behaviors like cutting be a sign of mental illness?

3. Those with miraculous powers were able to cast out demons. How were miraculous powers imparted? Read Acts 8:14-18.

4. Why was David running from King Saul?

5. Are you in a safe space emotionally to read the next chapter on suicide? If not, take a break or skip to the next chapter, and then come back to the chapter on suicide later.

"The spirit of a man will sustain him in sickness, but who can bear a broken spirit?"

(Proverbs 18:14)

4

SUICIDE IN THE SCRIPTURES

My niece had just gotten home from school. When asked how her day was and she began explaining, the emotional flood gates opened. She was sobbing over a sixth-grade classmate, who had shown her a picture he had drawn of a gravestone with his name on it. He had confided in her that he wanted to die and said, "I don't want to be here." Stunned, my niece tried to calm him as he cried. She was very kind to the boy and did her best to encourage him, but to no avail. So, she alerted her teacher and got help for her classmate. Suicidal thoughts can affect anyone—even eleven-year-olds.

Nobody really likes to talk about death that much. It is a grim topic. When it comes to death by suicide, the tendency to shirk at such a discussion is even greater. Yet in 2020, in the United States, there were nearly twice as many suicides (45,979) as homicides (24,576), according to the Center for Disease Control and Prevention (CDC).[5] They also report that the second leading cause of death among people between the ages of 10 and 34 in the United States is suicide. It affects many individuals and families – even Christians – and it needs to be discussed.

---

5 National Institute of Mental Health (2021). *Suicide.* Accessed July 5, 2022. https://www.nimh.nih.gov/health/statistics/suicide.shtml.

Suicide Defined

Suicidal thinking, consideration, or planning is known as suicidal ideation. It can include planning one's own death or thinking about one's own death. Passive thoughts about dying or no longer wanting to "be here" are also a part of suicidal ideation. Whether many of us want to admit it or not, we have all, at times, thought about our own deaths. Or we may have had a bad day when we felt like it would be better if we were in heaven with the Lord. An individual does not have to have an active plan to end her life to be engaging in suicidal ideation.

The National Institute of Mental Health defines "suicide" as death caused by self-directed injurious behavior with intent to die as a result of that behavior.[6] Death-by-suicide is not something that just started happening in recent years. It has been prevalent throughout the ages that we can even observe several examples of it in the Bible.

Deaths by Suicide in the Bible

In the Bible, there are six recorded deaths by suicide. Everyone is familiar with Judas Iscariot—the one who sold Jesus out for thirty pieces of silver. And afterwards, it seems he could not live with what he had done. He tried to return the blood money that he received in exchange for betraying our Lord. *"Then he threw down the pieces of silver*

---

[6] National Institute of Mental Health (2021). *Suicide.* Accessed July 5, 2022. https://www.nimh.nih.gov/health/statistics/suicide.shtml.

in the temple and departed and went and hanged himself" (Matthew 27:5).

Then there was Samson. Before Samson was born, the Angel of the Lord appeared to his mother and said,

> *"For behold, you shall conceive and bear a son. And no razor shall come upon his head, for the child shall be a Nazirite to God from the womb; and he shall begin to deliver Israel out of the hand of the Philistines"* (Judges 13:5).

Because Samson lived according to the Nazirite vow, the Lord was with him, and he was very strong. But his wife Delilah had been enticed by the rulers of the Philistines to discover the secret of his strength—and to tell them. She pestered him until he eventually told her.

> *"No razor has ever come upon my head, for I have been a Nazirite to God from my mother's womb. If I am shaven, then my strength will leave me, and I shall become weak, and be like any other man."*
>
> *When Delilah saw that he had told her all his heart, she sent and called for the lords of the Philistines, saying, "Come up once more, for he has told me all his heart." So, the lords of the Philistines came up to her and brought the money in their hand. Then she lulled him to sleep on her knees, and called for a man and had him shave off the seven locks of his head. Then she began to torment him, and his strength left him." (Judges 16:17-19).*

The Philistines then came and overtook Samson, gouged out his eyes, and threw him in prison. Later, they called for Samson while they were in the temple (Judges 16:25-27). Samson prayed to God and asked Him to give him strength one last time, so he could exact vengeance on the Philistines (Judges 16:28). Then Samson exerted so much force against the pillars of the temple that it collapsed on him and on the Philistines, crushing them all. The number of people that died that day was more than he had killed in his entire life.

In battle, King Saul and his armorbearer both deliberately fell on their swords in the face of impending death. (1 Samuel 31:4-5). Ahithophel, a trusted advisor to David, advised Absalom in his fight against his father King David, and then—when he realized how events had turned—Ahithophel killed himself (2 Samuel 17:23). And lastly, Israel's King Zimri reigned for seven days after conspiring against King Elah. When he realized the city had been captured, he ran into the palace and, while inside, burned it down. (1 Kings 16:18).

Dying by suicide is not new. It has been happening for a long time across different cultures and spans of time. That is why we should not be reluctant to talk about it – because it has happened one time too many.

Discuss Suicide Openly

If we more openly discuss death-by-suicide, people who are struggling with suicidal thoughts will be more likely to receive help. We need to remove this subject from the taboo-list. With more open discussion and less stigma, together we can flatten the curve of suicidal deaths.

Suicidal thinking and death by suicide can occur in any population, and suicidal thinking can lead to harming oneself. While there is no concrete evidence that Jesus was suicidal, even He was tempted to endanger His own life. Recall that when He was in the wilderness, the devil tempted Him to stand on the pinnacle of the temple and jump down from it (Matthew 4:5-6). The Bible clarifies that temptation is enticing because it draws toward our own desires (James 1:14). The devil tempted Jesus to test whether God would order His angels to protect Him (Luke 4:10). And Jesus was in all points tempted as we are (Hebrews 4:15). Not even Christ was exempt from temptation that could have physically harmed Him. If Jesus was tempted to put His life in danger - even if it was not associated with suicidal thinking – then we can be inclined to do the same.

Again, passive thoughts of suicide are probably more common. That includes the pondering of what-if-I-just-don't-wake-up type of thoughts. It is important to note that even though Jesus Christ was tempted to endanger His life, He did not carry out the act. He chose to resort to the Word of God. He told the devil, *"It is written again, 'You shall not tempt the Lord your God'"* (Matthew 4:7). And that's exactly how we should respond to any temptation—by employing the Word of God and speaking what God says. We have a wonderful example to follow in Jesus Christ.

Jesus Christ was described as a Man of sorrows, who was acquainted with grief (Isaiah 53:3). He took on our grief and our sorrows so that we would not have to carry them alone.

Suicide is a serious concern, even within Christendom. Protestants may have the highest suicide rate, but specific data in that area is lacking. Believing in Christ does not disqualify one from having emotions, from becoming depressed, or from experiencing a chemical imbalance that can negatively impact one's thinking. We will look at some warning signs in recognizing suicidal behavior and thinking in Chapter 6.

There is Always Hope

We must know that suicidal thinking can be overcome. If Jesus overcame, so can we. He said, *"In the world you will have tribulation; but be of good cheer, I have overcome the world"* (John 16:33).

If you or anyone you know is contemplating suicide, just remember that no one is ever really alone. Jesus declared, *"I will never leave you nor forsake you"* (Hebrews 13:5). There is hope, there is healing, and there is strength to make it to a brighter day. The Lord provides that kind of comfort to anyone in need. He says, *"Fear not, for I am with you; be not dismayed, for I am your God. I will strengthen you, yes, I will help you. I will uphold you with My righteous right hand"* (Isaiah 41:10).

Questions for Reflection

1. What is the first recorded suicide in the Bible? Did God condone it? List the Scripture reference here.

2. Do a little research. What is the National Suicide Prevention Lifeline?

3. Why do you think the suicide rate is significantly higher than the homicide rate?

4. Read Proverbs 6:16-17. What does God hate as it relates to suicide?

5. Is suicide a sin? Read Romans 9:15-18. Can a person definitively say that one who dies by suicide is condemned? What does God say about it?

6. Use a concordance to locate three Scriptures to share with someone who is depressed or suicidal.

PART II:

HELPING PEOPLE WITH MENTAL HEALTH CONDITIONS

“Nor give heed to fables and endless genealogies, which cause disputes rather than godly edification which is in faith.”

(1 Timothy 1:4)

5

DEBUNKING MYTHS

Stop it! You're scaring my children" my sister exclaimed. I thought, *"Stop what, and how?!"* I would never intentionally do anything to frighten or hurt my nieces or nephews. So, to hear her say that hurt my heart.

My sister was referring to me walking around our shared home, looking for hidden cameras. The kids naturally asked what I was doing, and I told them. So, they followed me—it became the looking-for-hidden-cameras game. I didn't think that I was scaring them. My paranoia about someone watching me was not something I could turn off and on. What was I to do? I did not know how to stop being how I was or stop thinking like I was thinking.

Thinking I had scared the children caused me great consternation. I became severely depressed. I did not want to do anything that had negative effects on the people that I loved the most, yet I could not stop being who I was. I could not change my thinking. But my sister was sure I could easily stop believing I was being watched and stop talking about it.

Myths Perpetuate a Culture of Fear

The prevalence of ill-informed ideas circulating about mental illness is one reason why talking about mental health issues remains so taboo. Myths surrounding mental illness perpetuate fear in individuals experiencing mental health concerns and those around them because people fear the unknown. And most people are unequipped with knowledge about mental health. Individuals afflicted by mental illness and their families can better address their issues if they have a correct knowledge and understanding of the issues they face.

Myth #1: People afflicted with mental illness are weak or weak-minded.

Having a mental health condition is not equivalent to having a lack of strength or a lack of mental fortitude. In fact, it takes ample courage for a person to acknowledge her symptoms and admit that she is dealing with a mental illness.

Still—at some level, out of my awareness—I believed the ugly myth about weakness. So, it took me a while to come to terms with my mental illness. People close to me kept telling me about symptoms they noticed. My friends and family kept thinking I needed help. But I was determined that I could overcome those symptoms on my own if I worked hard enough. I thought I could do it if I put forth a considerable effort.

But no matter how hard I tried, there were some things I just could not fix on my own. You see, it was not about my strength. I had plenty of strength. What really took strength was recognizing that I did have a mental illness, and that I could not fix it by myself. If a person has cancer or diabetes, they require treatment by trained medical professionals. No matter how much a woman tries, no matter how strong she is, she cannot cure the illness on her own. The same is true for mental illness. If someone is sick in her mind, it has nothing to do with physical or mental strength or her will power.

Myth #2: Christians who are mentally ill are not spiritual or spiritual enough.

In reality, many mental illnesses can be attributed to a chemical imbalance in the brain. Being sick in the mind or brain does not make a person less spiritual any more than being sick physically would affect a person's spirituality. If anything, it may cause someone to become closer to or depend more on the Lord for strength to endure her afflictions. A person's maladies—physical or mental—do not directly correlate to their relationship with God.

Consider Job. He was a man who feared God and hated evil—a righteous man (Job 1:1). He faced many mental and physical challenges at the hands of Satan. Yet, the Bible calls him blameless before God.

Remember the woman with the blood-flow issue in Mark 5:25-34? She had been sick for twelve years, and when she heard about Jesus and His miraculous power to heal, *"she came behind Him in the crowd and touched His garment. For she said, 'If only I may touch His clothes, I shall be made well'"* (Mark 5:27-28). Jesus told her that her faith had made her well (Mark 5:34). In this woman, we see someone not being well and drawing closer to the Lord because of it.

There are several more examples of devout men and women in the Bible, who were afflicted with mental illnesses. Remember Hannah? She was depressed and would not even eat. Nevertheless, her depressive state caused her to pray to the Lord in her anguish (1 Samuel 1:10). Jeremiah was a prophet of God, who became down and discouraged. He prayed to God, wishing that he had never been born (Jeremiah 20:14-18). We even observed that Jesus Christ, the Holy Son of God, was tempted with suicide. So, an individual who experiences mental illness should not unquestionably be deemed less spiritual than someone who is considered mentally healthy. (We do need to be careful here to not say that Jesus had a mental illness. I think that would be a stretch.)

Myth #3: People who take medicine for their mental illness want an easy fix.

We will address this more in Chapter 9, but I am a counterexample to the myth, making it untrue. Contrary to the myth, some mental illnesses cannot be managed without medication. I cannot stand taking medicine. I simply loathe the idea of putting chemicals into my body, when I could be, otherwise, helped in some natural way. Not everyone wants an easy fix.

Most people who are sick just want to become well and will do what it takes to be whole again. Whoever said taking medicine was easy, anyway? I do not know of anyone who actually wants to be obligated to take medication every single day of her life. A lot of people who have a mental illness struggle more because they detest taking medicine. Just because medication can come in a small capsule form does not make it an easy fix.

Myth #4: Discussing suicide with someone will make them suicidal or have suicidal thoughts.

You will not put thoughts of suicide in someone's head by asking if they are suicidal. We ask so we can help. By asking the question, you are more likely to stop someone from carrying out suicide.

If someone is actively considering suicide, and a friend or loved one asks about it outright, she will probably admit it. No one knows what is in the spirit of a person unless he or she tells him (1 Corinthians 2:11). It is better to inquire and spark a dialogue about it than to be on the other side of a death-by-suicide, having never brought up the discussion.

In the next chapter we will study signs to help identify a friend or loved one who may be suicidal.

Questions for Reflection

1. What are some other myths about mental illness and people who experience it?

2. Why is taking medicine not always an easy fix?

3. Why do some people with mental illnesses hate the idea of taking medication to treat their conditions?

4. Read Jeremiah 20:14-18:

   "Cursed be the day in which I was born! Let the day not be blessed in which my mother bore me! Let the man be cursed Who brought news to my father, saying, 'A male child has been born to you!' Making him very glad. And let that man be like the cities which the Lord overthrew, and did not relent; Let him hear the cry in the morning And the shouting at noon, because he did not kill me from the womb, that my mother might have been my grave, and her womb always enlarged with me. Why did I come forth from the womb to see labor and sorrow, that my days should be consumed with shame?"

   Why was Jeremiah depressed?

5. How might serving in the church and being spiritually focused sometimes lead a person into depression?

"A merry heart makes a cheerful countenance, but by sorrow of the heart the spirit is broken."

(Proverbs 15:13)

6

NOTICING SIGNS OF SUICIDAL IDEATION & HAVING A SAFETY PLAN

It was three in the morning. With tears streaming down my face, I grabbed my phone and texted three of my dearest friends to thank them for their friendship. I had already counted a variety of at least 100 prescription and over-the-counter pills and I placed them by my side. As I lay there in mental anguish typing the words, I did not expect anyone to reply.

If I had expected them to reply, I would not have sent the messages. I figured they would all be asleep and view the messages when they woke. But everyone responded—and right away. They could tell something was wrong, and they all knew what my message meant: I was saying goodbye.

Saying goodbye to friends or family is one of the signs of suicidal thinking. It can be subtle, but my friends were already aware of my tendencies to contemplate my own death. No matter how I tried to veil the signs, they knew me and my illness well enough to recognize the signs. And they all sent me comforting messages there in the dark of that night. One friend, in particular, talked through the pain with me.

Having someone to talk to, to listen, and to try and understand what I was going through helped pull me out of a deep, dark pit of despair.

Knowing the Signs

Knowing the signs of suicidal ideation is important. You can save a life if you know what to look for in a friend or loved one who may be suicidal.

Warning signs in *speech* include: discussing death; being preoccupied with dying; expressing ideas about being burdensome to others; voicing thoughts about being trapped or feeling there are no solutions; or saying goodbye to friends and family. Some people will start discussing funeral planning or begin pondering out loud how it might be when they die. Suicidal people may continually apologize for being a burden or feel they can't fix their problems. Hopelessness begins to set-in. For me it was feeling that I had no way to solve the issues that I faced—no matter how I tried to fix them. I discussed those issues with anyone I thought I could trust, until I just got so tired of talking about them because nothing seemed to help.

Warning signs in *behavior* include: stocking up pills; researching or purchasing a gun unexpectedly; extreme changes in moods from depression to sudden happiness; use of drugs or alcohol; changes in eating or sleeping habits; isolating oneself and avoiding or withdrawing from loved ones; or planning to give away or giving away belongings.[7]

When you recognize the signs in someone you love, it is imperative that you take action. It can be as simple as asking the question, "Are you thinking about killing yourself?" Do not be afraid to talk about suicide with someone you suspect is struggling with intentions about it. It is better to ask on the side, where he is still alive than, later, to wonder what you could have done to prevent his death.

Suicide can happen to anyone at any age. It affects children as young as six and octogenarians. It affects people of all races and socioeconomic statuses. Some may argue that they would never carry out suicide or even think about it. But nobody is excluded.

Preventing Suicide

This is why we must all play a role in preventing suicide. You never know what may happen to you or how you might react to it. Trauma is a major causative factor in many mental illnesses—and not just Post-Traumatic Stress Disorder (PTSD). A traumatic experience can lead to suicidal thinking, as well. We have to be prepared for what may come.

I strongly recommend that everyone develops a Suicide Safety Plan. Jesus said, *"For which of you, intending to build a tower, does not sit down first and count the cost, whether*

---

7 National Institute of Mental Health (2021). *Suicide Prevention.* Accessed July 4, 2022. https://www.nimh.nih.

he has enough to finish it" (Luke 14:28). Then He said, *"Or what king, going to make war against another king, does not sit down first and consider whether he is able with ten thousand to meet him who comes against him with twenty thousand?"* (Luke 14:31). Jesus knew the importance of planning.

We are essentially trying to build a wall against suicide, so it doesn't happen. We are fighting against strongholds; we are in a war. And we must sit down soberly, consider the cost, and plan ahead so that we can win the fight.

Just like having a fire-escape plan in your home or on your job, a safety plan for suicide can come in handy, just in case it is needed. Families should discuss their plans or complete them together.

Making A Suicide Safety Plan

Making a plan is simple:

1. Grab a sheet of paper (or use the template at the end of this chapter).
2. Write the heading *Warning Signs.*
3. List three or four signs or symptoms that would be specific for you. For some people sleeping too much, or drinking alcoholic beverages, or not eating may be warning signs.
4. Create another heading, *Safe Environment.*
5. Under this heading, list items that need to be removed from your environment to make it safe. For instance, if there is a gun in your home, you would remove the gun. Or, if there is an excess number of pills, then you would remove them from your

environment. Expired and unneeded pills can be dropped off at police stations, fire stations, or hospitals for safe disposal. We do not want the chemicals going into our water table. Creating a safe environment could also mean removing toxic people from your life.

6. Create another heading: *Activities.*
7. List productive activities you can complete alone when you start to notice warning signs and symptoms. These might include reading the Bible, meditating, praying, gardening, exercising, or any other independent activity. If you plan ahead of time by listing the activities that you can do and might enjoy, then when the time comes where you are not thinking normally, you can refer to your safety plan and have activities already designated to complete. This will help take your mind off suicidal intentions and refocus your attention to something productive.
8. Create a heading for *Contacts.*
9. List three or four people you can contact to help you when you are feeling suicidal. List their names and their phone numbers. Again, when an individual is experiencing suicidal thoughts, she is not in a normal frame of mind. So, a person may not think there is anyone she can confide in. Or she may think no one will care. But if you have a safety plan available and already completed, then you can reach out to someone or everyone on your safety plan's contact list.

Lastly, a solid safety plan should include a list of *Professionals* to contact if you are feeling suicidal. These might include, but are not limited to, therapists, psychologists, psychiatrists, primary-care physicians, or other health professionals to contact in times of emergency. The number for the Suicide Prevention Lifeline should also be included. It is 1-800-273-8255 or 988. There is even a Text Crisis Line; all a person has to do is text *hello* to 741741.

10. Then, feel free to add anything else to your safety plan that may help you in a time of need.

Remember, we are planning for an emergency, so make the plan as specific as possible and tailored to your needs. For instance, my Suicide Safety Plan includes the activity: *Make a list of things for which you are grateful.* That is an activity that I can complete independently, and it helps me to change my perspective when I am feeling down.

We can help prevent suicide by implementing a Suicide Safety Plan. Below you will find an example of a Suicide Safety Plan. It will not take long to complete, and you will be happy that you did when the time arises when you or a loved one needs the plan. Make the conscious decision now to choose to live, despite how difficult the storms of life may be later. You can live. There is hope for a brighter day. There was hope for me there in the dark of night, and there is hope for you, too.

Questions for Reflection

1. What behaviors have you noticed in yourself or in others that may be deemed as warning signs of suicidal ideation?

2. Does the presence of signs or symptoms always indicate that suicidal thinking is present? For instance, can someone be sleeping more than normal because they took on extra shifts at work, and not necessarily be suicidal?

3. What are some independent activities that you can engage in when you are feeling down or depressed?

4. What are the pros to completing a Suicide Safety Plan?

5. Read Luke 14:28-32:

   "For which of you, intending to build a tower, does not sit down first and count the cost,

whether he has enough to finish it— lest, after he has laid the foundation, and is not able to finish, all who see it begin to mock him, saying, 'This man began to build and was not able to finish'? Or what king, going to make war against another king, does not sit down first and consider whether he is able with ten thousand to meet him who comes against him with twenty thousand? Or else, while the other is still a great way off, he sends a delegation and asks conditions of peace."

What does the Bible teach about planning? How does the above Scripture correlate with the imperative of developing a Suicide Safety Plan?

SUICIDE SAFETY PLAN

Warning Signs - List the warning signs that you need to be on the lookout for:

1. ____
2. ____
3. ____

Safe Environment - What do you need to remove from your environment to make it safe for you?

1. ____
2. ____
3. ____

Activities - List productive activities that you can complete when you start to notice warning signs and symptoms.

1. ____
2. ____
3. ____

Contacts - List 3 people (or more with their phone numbers) that you can contact if you are feeling suicidal.

1. ____
2. ____
3. ____

Professionals - List the names and numbers of therapists, doctors, psychiatrists, or other professionals who you can contact in case of an emergency.

1. ____
2. ____
3. ____

“Anxiety in the heart of man causes depression, but a good word makes it glad.”

(Proverbs 12:25)

7

ENCOURAGING THE CHRONICALLY DEPRESSED

Earlier, I mentioned how I had gone through a deep depression during my divorce. That major loss was compounded by the devastating loss of my sweet grandmother, and I had made a significant change in my career by leaving the teaching profession, as well. So multiple factors resulted in a major depression.

One day as I drove to a counseling appointment, I was so sad I could not keep from crying. I lost focus and hit the bumper of the car in front of me. (There was only a scratch on the woman's car. But of course, she called for the whole nine yards—ambulances and neck braces for her and her kids. It was kind of laughable, knowing that I had just barely tapped her bumper. But I was not laughing that day.) The point is that a pervading sadness had engulfed me, and I had lost my ability to concentrate, causing me to have a car accident.

Everyone experiences discouragement sometimes. But people with depression have more persistent symptoms.

Their symptoms interfere with activities of daily living and thus their ability to serve and work in the church, on their jobs, and in their families. Take, for instance, the mother who just had a baby. She may oversleep or not eat enough food. She may be drained of energy more than usual for a new mother. She might even begin to miss the services of the church. Her symptoms are not that different from someone who experiences depression. When we see people hurting, we want to help them. But it is not always easy to know what to say and how to say it.

Be Helpful Not Harmful

When someone is depressed and we recognize it, we have to be careful not to say things that might be more harmful than helpful. Never advise a friend or loved one to "Get over it." It comes across as extremely callous and unsympathetic. Plus, if it were that easy, she probably would have "gotten over it" on her own without someone imploring her.

Never tell someone who is depressed or mentally ill, "You're crazy." That verbal jab probably stings more than any other. A few people have said those hurtful words to me or about me, and I still cringe just thinking about it. Telling someone they are crazy will decrease her level of trust in you and hinder any opportunity to genuinely help her. Imagine Jesus in the Garden of Gethsemane praying and then coming out to His disciples, asking them to watch and pray with Him. What if they had said to Jesus, "Get over it!" or "You're crazy"? I'm not saying that Jesus was struggling with a mental illness, but He was struggling with the reality that He was about to die an excruciating death and taking on the punishment of my sin and your sin, He would be cut off from God the Father. It is hard for us to fathom, but Jesus must have understood the full extent of that horror (Matthew 26:36-46). He wanted His friends to be on guard and pray with Him. That is what people who have a mental illness want from their friends.

Miserable Comforters

Let's consider Job again. He had all the reasons to be depressed, if ever there were any. He had lost his children, his sheep, his cattle, his health, and his wealth. His wife advised him to curse God and die. He sat on the ground in ashes scraping the boils from his skin. When his friends Bildad, Eliphaz and Zophar came to visit, they sat on the ground with him in silence for days. *"So they sat down with him on the ground seven days and seven nights, and no one spoke a word to him, for they saw that his grief was very great"* (Job 2:13). They were simply there for him.

But once they started talking, they began accusing Job, saying he must have done something wrong to have had such affliction come upon him. However, Job did not bite his tongue in telling his friends how he felt about them at the time. He said to them, *"I have heard many such things; miserable comforters are you all!"* (Job 16:2).

Instead of encouraging Job, his friends were indicting him for sins that he had not committed. He needed his friends to lift him up and give him hope, but they were failing. Miserably.

I imagine they had all the good intentions in the world toward Job. Yet, they conveyed their intentions in the wrong way. We can be guilty of doing the same thing if we are not careful. We do not want to be miserable comforters or to beat our family members or friends over the head with what they need to do or should have done.

You also do not want to announce to the depressed person: "You're not trying hard enough" or "You need to pray harder" or "Where is your trust in God?" These all perpetuate myths that a person who is mentally ill is not spiritual enough, strong enough, or close enough to God. It is not wise to assume that someone does not trust God or that she is not praying or praying hard enough because she is depressed.

Case Study of Prophet Elijah

Remember the prophet, Elijah? He was depressed because Jezebel sought to kill him (1 Kings 19:2-3). Elijah ran for his life, and he prayed to the Lord that he might die (1 Kings 19:4). Then he lay down and slept.

God had a remedy for Elijah's depression. He supplied him with food and told him to get up and eat (1 Kings 19:5). Then God allowed him to rest (1 Kings 19:6). Elijah then isolated himself and went into a cave and spent the night there (1 Kings 19:9). He was sorely depressed. God had to ask him what he was doing in a cave. Then God revealed Himself to Elijah and employed him to do a job (1 Kings 19:15-16). The case study of Elijah demonstrates a way to help those who are depressed.

When a friend or loved one is depressed and not eating, you can make sure she has food. This might mean a simple invitation to take her out to lunch or delivering her a meal. This could go a long way in supporting your friend or loved one. When someone is depressed, she is usually not thinking about carrying out normal activities of daily living—like eating. So, fixing a meal or taking the individual out to lunch might be helpful.

God also allowed Elijah time to rest. We can help Christians who are depressed by doing things that will ease their stress and allow them to relax. For the new mother struggling with depression, it might mean sitting with the baby for a few hours while the mother rests. For the depressed individual, encouraging her could include assisting in cleaning her home, washing her car, or taking care of something that would otherwise consume more of her energy.

Then God revealed Himself to Elijah and gave him work to do. We can support those who are experiencing depression by revealing Jesus and His loving, saving power to them. If someone you love is depressed and they do not know Christ as their Savior, now is as good a time as any to tell them how they can be saved and experience the blessings of Christ. You can offer to study the Bible with them and show them Scriptures like Ephesians 1:3 that explain how all spiritual blessings are in Christ—that includes love, joy, peace of mind, and salvation. Then show them Galatians 3:27 that tells us that we are baptized into Christ. In this way, you can demonstrate through the Scriptures that they can obtain the blessings that Christ has to offer by being baptized. They can be saved like Mark 16:16 states: *"He who believes and is baptized will be saved; but he who does not believe will be condemned."*

You can also make a point to discuss with your loved one the goodness of the Lord. Remind them, gently, of all the good in their lives and that God is the giver of all good gifts. Lastly, you can aid your friend or loved one in finding something productive to do. Things you may want to say include: "Can we pray together?" or "Would you like to study the Bible with me?" When you really work to encourage those who are depressed, you will more than likely be encouraged yourself.

Using The Right Words

Using the right words can be difficult to do at times. But we are commanded: *"Let your speech always be with grace, seasoned with salt, that you may know how you ought to answer each one"* (Colossians 4:6). That means that our speech is to be favorable and attractive to the hearer. And salt adds flavor, so the words that we speak should add a noticeable quality to the lives of others around us.

There is life and death in the power of the tongue. *"Even so the tongue is a little member and boasts great things. See how great a forest a little fire kindles!"* (James 3:5). One of the smallest parts of our bodies can have a huge impact on someone else's life and our own.

The Bible says, *"With it we bless our God and Father, and with it we curse men, who have been made in the similitude of God. Out of the same mouth proceed blessing and cursing. My brethren, these things ought not to be so"* (James 3:9-10).

The words that we speak can either be a blessing or bring harm, so we must be mindful of the things that we say to someone struggling with a mental illness. Let each of us choose to be a blessing in the way that we speak.

As you wrestle with what to say to those that may be struggling with mental illness, consider some of the following suggestions:

What to Say

- Can we pray together?
- Would you like to study the Bible with me?
- What can I do to be of help to you?
- I understand you are experiencing a difficult time.
- Would you like to visit the sick/widows/shut-ins with me?
- I have some extra cards; would you like some to send to those on the prayer/sick list with me? It may help you feel better.

What Not to Say

- You're not trying hard enough.
- You need to pray harder.
- Where's your trust in God?
- You're crazy.
- Get over it.

Questions for Reflection

1. Read 1 Kings Chapter 19. While the text does not say explicitly that Elijah was depressed, what symptoms did he display to show that he was?

2. Notwithstanding the list provided above, what are some other things that you should not say to someone who is depressed?

3. What other things should you say?

4. When Jesus was agonizing over his impending death in the Garden, what did He say to His closest friends? Read Matthew 26:40-41.

5. What can you do to make sure you're not a miserable comforter?

6. When you experienced a difficult time in your life, how did others encourage you? List three Scriptures that might be helpful to share with someone who is experiencing depression.

"And do not seek what you should eat or what you should drink, nor have an anxious mind."

(Luke 12:29)

8

ASSISTING ANXIETY-RIDDEN SISTERS

As I approached the doors to the church's auditorium, I thought: *Can I make it through this?* I was concerned about being able to participate in a full worship service because my anxiety about being around people and being in public was so bad that I could barely sit through a prayer, let alone a sermon.

Thankfully, my therapist is God-fearing and had a great solution to this problem. He explained how I needed to change my thinking before I even arrived at the building. He astutely pointed out that Jesus is always with me, and because of that, I had no reason to be afraid. He told me to imagine Jesus sitting next to me in the car as I drove, then Him walking beside me as I made my way to the building. Finally, he said to picture Jesus sitting next to me on the pew all throughout the worship service. With Jesus beside me, I had nothing to worry about.

My therapist was right. With Jesus by my side, my anxiety dissipated, and I was able to attend worship service. Whether I pictured Him or not, Jesus was always with me (and He still is), helping me through my troubles, into His peace and joy. I just had to become aware of it.

Overcoming Anxiety

Jesus said,

> *"Come to Me, all you who labor and are heavy laden, and I will give you rest. Take My yoke upon you and learn from Me, for I am gentle and lowly in heart, and you will find rest for your souls. For My yoke is easy and My burden is light" (Matthew 11:28-30).*

He wants us to have peace and rest in our souls. And anxiety is the opposite of peace and rest. We are commanded to not be anxious—the same way we are commanded not to be drunken—so there must be a way to overcome our anxieties. And there is. God would not command us to do something we are not capable of doing as we live in connection with Jesus.

Remember how Martha was troubled about many things? She was anxious. (Luke 10:41). Yet, Mary chose the better part, which was to sit at Jesus' feet. God wants *us* to choose the better part, as well, and to sit at Jesus' feet and learn from Him through the Word of God. We will be less anxious if we spend time studying the Bible. Studying with sisters who are anxiety-ridden can be an extremely effective method to assist them.

For people who are afflicted with an extreme mental illness, it is difficult for them to reason about normal day-to-day routines such as eating, sleeping, and even studying and reading their Bibles. So, one way to help is to offer to have a Bible study with a sister who is struggling. It does not have to be an elaborate study, and you do not have to be a Bible-class teacher to study the Bible with someone. The study could be as simple as reading through one or some of the Bible passages discussed in this book and answering the questions about them. This will help the anxious sister to reframe her mental processing and place her mind back on the Creator God, who can solve any problem.

Anxiety is the result of fear of a threat coupled with the doubt of ability to handle that threat. The more harm or danger the person assesses to himself and the assessed probability that it will happen, the higher the levels of fear and anxiety will be. If the person has no tools or resources to handle that perceived threat—which may present as real or imagined—then the level of anxiety in that person will be higher.

Addressing Negative Self-Talk

Addressing negative self-talk can reduce the perceived level of harm or danger. Some forms of negative self-talk include catastrophizing. It is the type of thinking that yields a catastrophic outcome. For instance, if I am prone to have panic attacks when I go to the grocery store (which I am not anymore; thank God, I have overcome them), then before I get to the store, I might speculate that I will have a panic attack, will not be able to breathe, and then die. That's a catastrophe. Most people, even anxious people, visit the store without any issues, gather their groceries, and return home alive and unharmed.

Other types of negative self-talk that contribute to anxiety can be identified in what David Burns calls Cognitive Distortions.[8] These include: having an all-or-nothing mindset, overgeneralizing, discounting the positive, jumping to conclusions, magnification or minimization, using "should" statements, and reasoning emotionally. You can lay a stepping stone to help anxious sisters reframe their mental processing and manage their anxiety. One way is to help them recognize when they are engaging in negative self-talk. You can help them reflect on their thinking. A practical way to accomplish this is to provide a counterstatement to every negative statement that they express. Gently challenging them to provide a counterstatement for their own negative self-talk is also effective in eliminating such behaviors.

For instance, if a sister laments, "I am never going to get better. Everything bad always happens to me," you may counter with, "You can get better. There is some good that has happened to you." Then challenge the sister to make her own counterstatement each time she recognizes that she is engaging in negative self-talk.

Self-Care

Some negative self-talk and anxiety can be rooted in self-esteem issues. You can try to address mistaken beliefs

---

8 Burns, David. *The Feeling Good Handbook.* New York: Plume, (1999).

that a sister may have about herself, but she must put forth the effort to have esteem and respect for herself. Recommend that she partake in activities that demonstrate self-care. That could be treating herself to a spa for a massage, visiting the hair salon for a new do, or painting her nails. Taking a long hot bath and reading a good book are also ways to show self-love and care. You do not have to spend money to take care of yourself.

You might invite a sister struggling with anxiety to a yoga or spin class. Or if she is not comfortable due to the possible crowd of people, you might suggest venturing outside for a walk. Exercise can be a powerful tool to reduce stress and anxiety, and it promotes healthy self-esteem.

Helping a sister with anxiety can be as simple as recommending that she attend psychotherapy or visit a psychiatrist or her doctor about medication. There are tools and resources available to assist with anxiety.

First and foremost, the Lord is able to bring us through anything. His Word says that *"many are the afflictions of the righteous, but the Lord delivers him out of them all"* (Psalm 34:19). God can and will deliver us from anxiety. We just have to be sure to use what He has given us to do so. We are not alone in our double-quest to be well and to help those in need.

Questions for Reflection

1. All-or-nothing thinking is characterized by no gray areas; everything is either good or bad, yes or no, right

or wrong. What are some examples of all-or-nothing thinking?

2. What are some patterns of negative self-talk you've noticed in yourself or others? How can you, or they, reframe that type of thinking?

3. Read Jonah chapter four. What was Jonah's negative self-talk? How did God work to reframe his thinking?

4. Give another example of someone in the Bible who engaged in negative self-talk. What did they say?

5. What self-care activities do you regularly schedule for yourself? List additional self-care activities not previously mentioned in this chapter.

PART III:

RESOURCES FOR THOSE STRUGGLING WITH MENTAL ILLNESSES

"A merry heart does good, like medicine; but a broken spirit dries the bones."

(Proverbs 17:22)

9

NOT A QUICK-FIX: TAKING MEDICATION

Rocking back and forth with my head in my hands, tears streaming down my face, I cried out to the psychiatric nurse, "I don't know what's real anymore!" The panic, the feelings of helplessness, and the immediate sense of danger were all so pressing. I had driven to the behavioral clinic's office without even a phone call to see if an appointment was available. I needed to see someone and talk to somebody about what I was experiencing.

Thankfully, they were able to fit me in to see someone; I think it was because they could see I was in so much distress. One of her first questions was, "Are you taking your medication?" My answer was a resounding *no*. I proceeded to inform her why I did not take the medication. She wrote me another prescription for a different medication and advised that I take the next day or so off from work to rest. And I did not like feeling the way I did, so I took the medication, hoping to get some relief.

The Importance of Taking Medication

Nobody likes to take medicine. People who are sick desire to be well, but medicine is not always top on everyone's list when it comes to feeling better. I have never been a fan of taking medication and have always believed in some fashion or another that most medications cause more harm than good. My preference is a natural path. Despite that, I recognize that, sometimes, there is no way around taking medication.

Oftentimes, mental illness is a result of a chemical imbalance within the brain, and that balance can only be restored with the aid of medication. Antidepressants can decrease the symptoms associated with depression, and antipsychotics can bring back a sense of stability and reality to the person suffering from a psychotic illness.

Mistaken beliefs about medication tend to make most people shy away from medicine. There are some people who believe that Christians who take medication for mental illnesses are looking for an easy way out from their troubles and that they do not want to do the work involved in progressing toward wholeness and wellness. That is not the case, and I can attest to that.

Any doctor I have had who has prescribed me medicine knows how much I detest taking prescriptions. I believed that, if I worked hard enough, I could improve my conditions and the symptoms that they caused without taking pharmaceuticals.

Nearly three years passed before I realized the importance of medication and how it improved my mental health conditions. Medication is a resource for healthy management. Just like people take meds for diabetes, it is also crucial to take medication for depression, anxiety, other mood disorders, and psychotic disorders – as well as other mental illnesses.

A Biblical Take on Medicine

Sometimes, we will be on the encouraging end of urging someone who is afflicted with a mental illness to take her medications. Other times, we may be on the receiving end. Even the apostle Paul mentioned that it was acceptable to use medicine when needed. Recall how he encouraged Timothy to drink a little wine for his stomach (1 Timothy 5:23). He said, *"No longer drink only water, but use a little wine for your stomach's sake and your frequent infirmities."* Apparently, Timothy needed encouragement to take his medicine. There is nothing wrong with Christians taking medicine for their mental health conditions.

Even Solomon knew that medicine could be beneficial for a person, just like a merry heart is good for the soul (Proverbs 17:22). When taking medication for a mental illness, months may pass before a person becomes regulated on a particular prescription. Doctors and psychiatrists often need to adjust medicines to find the most effective treatment.

In my experience with psychiatric medications, my doctors prescribed different dosages of particular medications since the originally ordered dosages did not prove effective in my treatment. I fought taking medication, and I fought hard. One reason was as I stated earlier. I believed that I could manage my mental health issues by just going to counseling and working hard at trying to get better. That was not the case. I improved some, but I was not making as much progress as I needed in order to function properly.

Another reason I felt compelled to avoid medication was because of my paranoia. I believed that my counselor, psychiatrist, and doctor were all plotting against me. I presumed that I did not have a mental illness and they were simply attempting to make me agree that I had one. It makes sense to me that someone who is not sick does not need to take medicine.

As a result, it took my team of mental health professionals, all together, and my experiences to help me see that part of my mental illness was to believe that I did not have a mental illness. There was no conspiracy against me on the part of my mental health professionals. They were only aiming to assist me. But, at first, it was challenging for me to recognize this. No one could tell me any differently.

However, now I realize that I do have a mental illness, and I understand the importance of managing my mental illness with medication. Having to take medication is not the end of the world. It simply means you are sick and putting forth the effort to become better.

Those who were at the cross of Jesus attempted to provide Him some form of medicine, while He endured so much suffering and pain (Matthew 27:34). They tried to give Him sour wine mixed with gall, but when he tasted it, He would not drink it. According to Albert Barnes, "The drink, therefore was vinegar or sour wine, rendered 'bitter' by the infusion of wormwood or some other very bitter substance. The effect of this, it is said, was to stupefy the senses. It was often given to those who were crucified, to render them insensible to the pains of death."[9] Jesus refused the sour wine mixed with gall on the way to the cross. He had a cup to drink that the Father had given Him, and He chose to avoid dulling or numbing, in any way, the pain and suffering He had to endure for us.

Some psychiatric medications are like that today. One of the first medications I was prescribed had me zoned-out. After I ingested it, I could barely hold my eyes open, and when they were open, I was awake, but I was not really present in the moment. I was numb to everything and just wanted to sleep endlessly. That is not the kind of medicine that anybody needs. It could become habit-forming, like some benzodiazepines. Eventually and thankfully, I was taken off of that zoning-out prescription. A sister may have to try a few things before finding the fit that helps restore joy and purpose in her life.

For me, taking medicine was not and is not a sign of weakness. It took strength and courage to realize I could not manage my mental illnesses on my own and that I required the help of psycho-pharmaceuticals. It was quite the opposite of trying to take medicine as a quick fix, and for many the same is true. In fact, it often takes a humility

---

9 Bible Hub. 2022. *Matthew 27*. Accessed July 5, 2022. https://biblehub.com/commentaries/barnes/matthew/27.htm

that is godly, to recognize that one needs help. Medication is not the end-all-be-all or a panacea for all of one's mental-health conditions. It is, however, a potent resource in actively managing many mental illnesses.

Questions for Reflection

1. How were the wines mentioned in Matthew 27:34 and Matthew 27:48 different? See John 19:28-30.

2. Is the "wine" mentioned in 1 Timothy 5:23 similar to or different than the "wine" of Matthew 27:34? How so?

3. How is the "wine" that Paul told Timothy to take similar to some medicines that we take today?

4. Does Paul's instruction to Timothy to drink wine for his stomach give us a license to drink alcoholic beverages socially? Explain your answer with Scripture.

5. How can medication be an effective resource for someone afflicted with mental illness?

“Where there is no counsel, the people fall; but in the multitude of counselors there is safety.”

(Proverbs 11:14)

10

ONE WORD OF ADVICE: ATTEND COUNSELING OR PSYCHOTHERAPY

My first experience with psychotherapy was as a child. I would watch rich people of Caucasian descent portrayed as having to visit a "shrink" as a joke on television sitcoms. I did not think it was something normal that people—people who were not rich and white—did.

My eyes were opened to reality when I was in college and landed a job working in the Student Development Services Office. Housed within that office was a counseling center. From that point forward, I began to view psychotherapy in a different light. People from all walks of life would visit the office for counseling. I even had a friend who received counseling there. She often gushed about how much she loved her counselor and recommended him highly.

Similar to my thinking about counseling growing up, many people have misconceptions about receiving therapy. There are also cultural barriers that prevent many, especially minorities from seeking that kind of help. Yet, counseling is not solely for one group of people or a certain type of person, from a specific ethnic background.

Stigma Associated with Counseling

For some, there is a stigma associated with receiving counseling. Remember, my first memory of someone receiving counseling was as a joke—something that was laughable, not to be taken seriously, frowned upon, and mocked socially. But that was years ago.

Still, nearly three decades later, some individuals do not receive the care they need because of the shame associated with psychotherapy for mental health conditions. Many homes have an unspoken rule that issues must be handled within the family. Outside help is taboo. In some instances, that rule may work, but when it comes to a person's mental well-being, counseling is an excellent resource for making progress and improving one's conditions.

Most people will not hesitate to seek medical attention for their high cholesterol, hypertension, and other physical issues. But when it comes to mental illness, many take a pause. Receiving assistance for mental health issues when your mind is not well is analogous to receiving care for physical ailments when your body is not well.

There are licensed professional counselors and psychologists who are trained in treating illnesses and conditions of the mind. They can provide anyone who is suffering with a mental illness with tools and resources to assist her healing and to aid her to better cope with her conditions. It is wise to seek counsel, rather than try to wing it and improve on your own.

Seeking Wise Counsel

Solomon said it best: "*The way of a fool is right in his own eyes, but he who heeds counsel is wise*" (Proverbs 12:15). The Word of God instructs us that a person of understanding attains wise counsel (Proverbs 1:5). Seeking counseling as a resource in combating and treating a mental health concern is in the best interest of the individual afflicted with mental illness and those in her family, who are often affected, as well.

Finding good counsel can be difficult. Finding Christian counselors can be even more challenging. However, it is well worth the effort required to have godly counsel. Remember Psalm 1:1? *"Blessed is the man who walks not in the counsel of the ungodly."* Non-Christian counselors may have a worldview contrary to what Christ teaches, and that can direct their counseling style and how they treat certain conditions and issues. That is why it is crucial to ask potential counselors very pointed questions in the beginning to ascertain which approach they take toward counseling, and if they will be a good fit.

After consulting several counselors over the years, I have gained a skill in determining whether the counselor is a good fit for me in the initial consultation meeting. I have been to a counselor, who revealed that she did not want to be a counselor but preferred to be teaching. I have had a counselor reveal that he was Jewish, that his faith was important, and that it impacted how he viewed certain issues. I have also had a counselor pull out his cellphone, actually talk on the phone, and answer text messages in the middle of my session. You can find out valuable information about a counselor by asking questions and by being observant.

One might ask a counselor if she is religious and if so, whether her religious views take precedence in or influence her counseling. If you do not feel comfortable with a counselor after your first consultation, then do not go back.

One approach to therapy is some form of a cognitive-behavioral therapy. It focuses on changing the individual's behavior associated with the issue she is having by changing her thought processes. It was the apostle Paul who said that you are *"transformed by the renewing of your mind"* (Romans 12:2).

People Who Sought Counseling in the Bible

There are many biblical examples of people seeking counsel in the Bible. The prophet Nathan counseled Bathsheba in making her son Solomon the king to succeed David after Adonijah basically made himself king (1 Kings 1:1-14). Because she followed Nathan's counsel, David proclaimed Solomon as king, and Adonijah's plans were thwarted. King Zedekiah sought the prophet Jeremiah's counsel (Jeremiah 38:14-23). Jeremiah advised him to surrender to the king of Babylon's princes in order to save his life. King Rehoboam sought the counsel of his father Solomon's elders. He also desired, and unwisely followed, counsel from his young friends (1 Kings 12:6-8, 14).

It is not uncommon to seek the advice of others. If someone is struggling with anxiety, depression, or other mental illnesses, trained professionals have tools and resources to aid the individual in better coping with her mental health condition. Depending on the issue, the treatment that therapy provides can allow a person with a mental illness to become free of her mental health concerns.

Questions for Reflection

1. What are some preconceptions that you or others may have about counseling or psychotherapy?

2. Use a concordance to find two additional Bible verses that teach us it is wise to seek counsel.

3. Whose counsel did Rehoboam heed? And, what was the result of his decision?

4. Did King Zedekiah heed the counsel of Jeremiah? What happened to the king?

5. Who else in the Bible sought or gave counsel? List two examples.

"Come unto Me, all you who labor and are heavy laden, and I will give you rest."

(Matthew 11:28)

11

MORE THAN A BANDAGE: INPATIENT AND OUTPATIENT CARE

I was at a juncture in life where I had not taken my medications in months, my anxiety was at a high level, and I was extremely depressed. It was enough stress for me to realize that I needed help. So, I searched for mental health treatment facilities, where I could receive outpatient treatment to return to a point of functioning normally. I was not in the best space mentally. My work and general activities of daily living were becoming severely affected.

After researching psychiatric facilities in the area, I visited one to ask some questions and find out more information. The counselor completed a pre-assessment to determine if I met their criteria and whether their facility or services would fit my needs. After a thorough conversation, she recommended that I stay overnight, resume my meds, and leave the next day with a prescription. She indicated that, prior to being discharged, we could discuss outpatient treatment.

I voluntarily chose to stay. But by the time I was taken back to the residential area, I had decided that I did not trust my care to the people working there. I also did not trust being around all the people who were there for treatment. So, I stood up to walk out the door. The first door was open, but the second one was closed and locked. I turned around and asked the nurse to unlock the door. She refused. I told her that I had changed my mind and I was not staying. I turned back around to head towards the door, and she hit a button and shut the one that was open before I reached it. I was not allowed to leave, although I had walked in of my own volition.

Apparently, they believed that I needed to be there because they threatened to commit me if I did not calm down and stop trying to leave. But naturally I was upset since I had voluntarily walked into the facility and had people exclaiming to me that I could not walk back out the door.

Eventually, the counselor I had consulted with at the beginning came and spoke nicely and calmly with me. She explained to me the benefit of staying. What began as an overnight stay turned into nearly a week. But it was beneficial for me. I needed to start back on my medication and to have some time away from the hustle and bustle of life to refocus my mind to a more stable place.

Participating in art therapy, spending time alone, and consistently taking my medication aided me the most while I was at the facility. And I left feeling better than I did when

I arrived. I can say firsthand that inpatient care is invaluable.

The Good Samaritan

Remember the parable of the Good Samaritan? While traveling, a man was attacked and wounded by thieves. They took his clothing and left him on the side of the road for dead. *"But a certain Samaritan, as he journeyed, came where he was. And when he saw him, he had compassion. So he went to him and bandaged his wounds, pouring on oil and wine; and he set him on his own animal, brought him to an inn, and took care of him"* (Luke 10:33-34). The man he had helped was so badly hurt that he needed to be cared for at an inn. It was not just a matter of getting a bandage, hopping up again, and heading home. He needed extensive care.

Sometimes that is the way it is with a mental illness—intensive care is required. We go to the hospital if we break an ankle or if we become sick enough physically, without hesitation. But what about a broken spirit? What happens when the spirit of a person is broken to a point where no attempts to help have succeeded? It is then that inpatient care or intensive outpatient care may be needed to regulate the mental illness.

Intensive Care

Outpatient care can include psychotherapy. But more intensive outpatient care includes Monday through Friday treatment during the day. Group therapy, art therapy, and individual counseling are also part of the outpatient care experience. It resembles inpatient treatment in many ways, except for the fact that patients are allowed to travel back home at the end of the day.

Individuals who threaten or attempt suicide are prime cases for inpatient care. Providing a safe environment where they can be monitored and receive specialized treatment for their mental health is also paramount.

Similarly, inpatient care is critical when a person is psychotic and hearing voices. If someone begins to hear voices, those voices can tell him to do anything. He can present a danger to himself and others. Professional inpatient treatment is necessary to assist that individual in reaching a point of stability. Additionally, intensive outpatient or inpatient treatment may be required when a person has gone without their medication and is experiencing a major episode of decompensation.

Like the wounded man in the account of the Good Samaritan, it was necessary for me to have more than a bandage. I required intensive and extensive treatment. Not everyone will be willing to pursue inpatient or outpatient care. For those loved ones, who refuse that kind of treatment or do not see the need for it, you may offer a respite for them in your home.

A Respite for Care

When I was in distress, a number of times, two of my dear friends offered me a time away in their homes. I would drive five to seven hours and three states away to find a haven of rest away from my stressful environment and circumstances.

At one friend's home, I had the entire guest house to myself, and it brought me back to a place of peace and stability. This was especially helpful to be with loving friends when I experienced episodes of decompensation. While it is not a substitute for seeking professional medical treatment, time with friends, aside from life's everyday routines, can be advantageous to the individual struggling with a mental illness.

Recommending inpatient care for a friend or loved one may be needed, at times. There is nothing wrong with having to take care of your mental health. We do not see anything wrong with someone going to the hospital if they have a heart attack. In the same vein, when we are mentally ill, we need to seek treatment. It does not make one weak or less than the next person in any way. It actually makes a person strong and shows that they love themselves enough to seek help when needed.

Questions for Reflection

1. Why do you think the Good Samaritan couldn't just give the hurt man a bandage and then continue on about his way? Why did he have to take him to an inn?

2. What signs will you look for in yourself or a loved one to know that inpatient care or intensive outpatient care is needed?

3. How is intensive outpatient care different from a regular counseling or psychotherapy session?

4. Read Mark 6:31:

   > *"And He said to them, "Come aside by yourselves to a deserted place and rest a while." For there were many coming and going, and they did not even have time to eat."*

   What did Jesus tell His disciples to do? Why is this important?

5. Read John 6:15:

    "Therefore when Jesus perceived that they were about to come and take Him by force to make Him king, He departed again to the mountain by Himself alone."

    What did Jesus do when He perceived trouble coming His way? How is this similar to what He did when He found out that John the Baptist had died? See Matthew 14:10-23.

"When I remember You on my bed, I meditate on You in the night watches."

(Psalm 63:6)

12

BE WHOLLY HOLISTIC: OTHER TECHNIQUES FOR HEALING

I was a sickly child – in and out of hospitals and doctor's offices all the time. As a result of my childhood issues, I developed severe digestive problems. And as an adult, I went to doctor after doctor, specialist after specialist, in state after state, for procedure after procedure, and test after test. It was exhausting! And it was all to no avail. I received the same non-answers with new medications each time. Feeling defeated, I finally decided that something different had to be done in order to provide me with some relief.

So, I sought out naturopathic medicine. I also chose to completely change my diet and become a vegan. Then, I added exercise to my regimen. It was time to take a holistic approach for me, and not just focus on taking the medications prescribed to me for my digestive issues but to focus on my wellness as a whole. Similarly, when it comes to mental health, sometimes it takes more than medicine to provide relief from one's ailments. That is when a view of the disfunction in one's life must be approached on the level of body, mind, and spirit. Prayer, meditation, deep breathing, listening to music, and exercising can all be forms of healing to assist those with mental health concerns.

Exercise

There's nothing like hitting the pavement for a run, or clearing your mind on a walk. I often take walks throughout the day on my breaks at work. I spend that time in prayer to God and meditating on His Word. It gets me out of my chair and it gets me moving. It also aids me in calming my nerves when I get anxious about being in the office around several people. I am thankful to be able to have those times alone.

Exercise comes with many benefits. Although when compared to godliness, exercise profits little (1 Timothy 4:8), it still provides some benefit to the person who engages in it, including: effective weight management, weight loss, decreased blood pressure, and an increase in metabolic rate. Exercise is known to stimulate endorphins in the body, which are the "feel-good" compounds produced by the brain. They can help calm an anxious individual and help a depressed person feel better. According to Dr. Edmund Bourne, "Regular exercise has a direct impact on several physiological factors that underlie anxiety." [10] Exercise can also have a positive effect on

---

[10] Bourne, Edmund J. *The Anxiety and Phobia Workbook.* Oakland: New Harbinger Publications, Inc., 2015, 111.

people with other mental illnesses and on people who do not experience mental health issues.

One of the best things about exercise is that it does not require machines or leaving your home. There are various types of exercises like walking, jogging, yoga, weight lifting, and even cycling.

Prayer

Exercise can be a time of meditation. When you head out for a walk, you can use that as a time to pray to God, to clear your mind, or to collect your thoughts. Prayer is an effective communication tool. It pleases God when we pray, and it helps us to lay all our burdens at His feet.

I remember one night I stayed up all night praying to God. I was huddled in a corner on the floor of my bedroom facing the door almost in an upright fetal position. I felt so helpless, alone, and in despair. Soon, my prayer became short and repetitious. Then all I could pray was, "Lord, help me" until day broke, and I was able to fall asleep saying the same thing over and over. There were a few other words here and there, but that was the gist of it. It is times like that when the Scripture comes into play.

> *"Likewise, the Spirit also helps in our weaknesses. For we do not know what we should pray for as we ought, but the Spirit Himself makes intercession for us with groanings which cannot be uttered" (Romans 8:26).*

Thank God that the Holy Spirit intercedes for us and on our behalf. He was interceding for me that night and many other nights when I knew I needed help—I needed the Lord—and I just didn't know what kind of help I needed.

Many people think of prayers being long soliloquies with flowery words being prayed at the side of the bed on one's knees. But that is not always true. Our prayers are simply an avenue for us to commune with God. They do not have to be long and drawn out all the time (though there is absolutely nothing wrong with that). We can pray short prayers throughout the day. There is so much and there are so many people to pray for that we cannot get it all in one prayer.

Sometimes we are in a situation during our days that all we can pray is "Thank you, Father," or "Lord, help me." When we seriously don't know what to pray for, that is when the Holy Spirit steps in and intercedes for us. God is not concerned with our prayer portion—whether big or small. He wants us to communicate with Him.

The Lord is also not nitpicky about our prayer posture. It is not always possible to bow down on your knees when you pray. If you pray in the car, at work, or at a restaurant, then you will not be able to get down on your knees—not without causing a scene or a wreck. And Jesus does not want us bringing attention to ourselves when we pray. He said it clearly:

> *"But you, when you pray, go into your room, and when you have shut your door, pray to your Father who is in the secret place; and your*

> *Father who sees in secret will reward you openly" (Matthew 6:6).*

Jesus also taught His disciples, and by extension, He teaches us to not pray for others to see us:

> *"And when you pray, you shall not be like the hypocrites. For they love to pray standing in the synagogues and on the corners of the streets, that they may be seen by men. Assuredly, I say to you, they have their reward" (Matthew 6:5).*

Breathing

Breathing techniques can also assist with panic attacks, anxiety, racing thoughts, and other conditions. Slow, deep breathing from the diaphragm or the abdomen as opposed to shallow chest breathing can have a calming effect. I have often employed this method in many different places and at different times when I have felt anxious or panicked. You can do this at your desk at work, like I do, in church services, or at home in your bedroom. Mental health professionals recommend inhaling slowly while you feel the abdomen extend, then slowly exhaling. This can be done with a count of ten or twenty, or however long it takes to bring your body to a state of non-arousal.

Meditating

Meditating can also prove helpful in dealing with and managing mental health conditions. Meditation is more than just thinking about something. It involves mindful contemplation and reflection.

> *"This Book of the Law shall not depart from your mouth, but you shall meditate in it day and night, that you may observe to do according to all that is written in it. For then you will make your way prosperous, and then you will have good success" (Joshua 1:8).*

We can meditate on God's Word to help us through any situation.

The Bible says that the person who is blessed has her delight in the law of the Lord and she meditates in it day and night (Psalm 1:1-2). When we study God's Word and reflect upon it, it will aid us in our daily walk with Him.

When meditating, the individual suffering from a mental health concern should focus on the present moment and stop ruminating on the past or worrying about the future. Doing this for a specified amount of time can be a stress-management technique.

Regarding meditation, Dr. Edmund Bourne states, "If you suffer from an anxiety disorder, meditation can break up obsessional mental patterns and help you restructure your thoughts more productively."[11] He also pointed out that meditation has benefited those with major depression. Dr. Bourne provides some basic meditation exercises that can assist you in managing your stress and mental health conditions. I recommend his book *The Anxiety and Phobia*

---

[11] Bourne, Edmund J. *The Anxiety and Phobia Workbook.* Oakland: New Harbinger Publications, Inc., 2015, 425.

Workbook as an additional resource in managing mental health issues like anxiety and phobias.

Music

Listening to music is another tool for managing mental health conditions. Remember when King Saul was distressed in his spirit (1 Samuel 16:14-15). He may very well have been depressed. Saul called for David, and David played the harp for him whenever Saul was in distress (1 Samuel 16:23). Saul was calmed by the music David played for him. Music therapy is useful for a number of conditions. Music can bolster relaxation. Relaxation is not just binge-watching series on a streaming service, as some may contend. It involves activity that provides relief from your mental anxieties and conditions.

Exercising, praying, deep-breathing, meditating, and listening to music are effective forms of relaxation. Utilizing a number of methods aids in coping with mental illnesses like anxiety and depression. It is useful to know that medication is not the only respite from such troubles. It definitely is not a panacea, or cure-all, so we must take a holistic approach in managing stress and other disorders. Tools and resources are available. It just takes time and diligence to reap the benefits.

Questions for Reflection

1. What are some exercises you can do at home alone when you are feeling anxious or depressed?

2. How do you meditate on God's Word? What can you do differently to be a better meditator of his Word?

3. Is listening to Christ-centered music that is accompanied by instruments sinful? What about without mechanical instruments? Is it considered worship?

4. Read Colossians 3:16 and Ephesians 5:19. How do you make melody in worship?

5. What activities can you complete to glorify God in your relaxation?

"And if it seems evil to you to serve the Lord, choose for yourselves this day whom you will serve, whether the gods which your fathers served that were on the other side of the river, or the gods of the Amorites, in whose land you dwell. But as for me and my house, we will serve the Lord."

(Joshua 24:15)

13

JUST USE ME LORD: SERVING IN THE CHURCH WITH A MENTAL ILLNESS

When I first started my blog at christleadstheway.com, my motives were a bit selfish. I had begun to write as a means of therapy to combat my anxiety, depression, and paranoia. It was very helpful, too. As I wrote more and more about God, life, and the wonderful blessings God has bestowed upon me, I began to feel better. Little did I know I would reach thousands of people from several different countries on various continents.

I now write to fulfill the Great Commission and make disciples of all people, teaching them all things Christ has commanded. It is my prayer that Christ will be glorified in my writing on that blog, as well as this writing, and all the writing that I do. It is one way that I can serve Him.

And writing is something that I can do in the comfort of my own home. I do not have to worry about being around a lot of people or talking to anyone. It is just me and the keyboard. That works well for my anxiety and my paranoia – serving in that capacity.

Not everyone likes to write or can do it well, just like not everyone will prefer to visit shut-ins of the church or cook meals for those who need them. Remember the parable of the talents?

> *"For the kingdom of heaven is like a man traveling to a far country, who called his own servants and delivered his goods to them. And to one he gave five talents, to another two, and to another one, to each according to his own ability; and immediately he went on a journey. Then he who had received the five talents went and traded with them, and made another five talents. And likewise he who had received two gained two more also. But he who had received one went and dug in the ground, and hid his lord's money. After a long time the lord of those servants came and settled accounts with them" (Matthew 25:14-19).*

While the parable above is not talking about talents, as in gifts or abilities like we know the word to mean in our modern vernacular, the concept still applies. The Lord has given us all blessings according to our own abilities. And He does not want us to sit on them, hide them, or not use them. Just like no one lights a candle and puts it under a basket, we should not hide the blessings that the Lord gives to us but use them for good.

Mentally ill or not, you are the light of the world! *"Let your light so shine before men, that they may see your good works and glorify your Father in heaven"* (Matthew 5:16). We must use our "talents" for the good of others. In that way, we multiply them. And when the Lord returns for us in the day of judgment, He will settle His accounts with us to see what we have done with that which He has blessed us.

Commanded to Serve

We are commanded to be steadfast, immovable, always abounding in the work of the Lord (1 Corinthians 15:58). Yet things like anxiety, depression, posttraumatic stress disorder, and schizophrenia can interfere with a person's service to Christ. As I mentioned in an earlier chapter, I was not able to leave my home to attend church services because of agoraphobia, anxiety, and panic attacks. And when I was able to attend services, due to anxiety, I had to sit right by the door in case I needed to jet. So, you can imagine that my ability to serve with the church was significantly impeded. Others with similar conditions are likely to experience the same negative impacts to their service. However, God commands and expects everyone to serve Him. And opportunities to serve can aid in alleviating symptoms. For example, someone who is struggling with depression may start to feel better when she does something to help someone else.

Serving with Limitations Due to Mental Illness

Those struggling with mental illnesses need opportunities to serve in ways that are aligned with their functional limitations. A person with panic attacks or who is fearful of public spaces must limit her exposure to crowds. But having limitations does not make her less spiritual. Christians with mental health conditions still desire to serve God. They just have to serve Him and others in a less conventional manner or behind the scenes in order to limit interaction with people.

Grading and mailing Bible correspondence courses is a way to serve others and serve Christ. Not only will the correspondence courses benefit the student, they can promote spiritual growth in the grader, as well. Imagine the kinds of questions that students may ask that the responder will have to answer and, possibly, research to find the answer. It can also be a tool to aid in memorization, seeing the same courses and Scriptures continually.

Another area of service in the church for people who struggle with a mental illness is website development and maintenance. This requires little to no contact with people, yet church websites can be a resource to listen to previous sermons, to livestream services, and for members to interact with one another. With so many different software programs now available, it is easy to learn how to make a website and maintain it. I was able to create a church website and maintain it for the time that I was with a specific congregation. So, I know that it can be done and that many people can benefit from it.

There are usually a number of people on the church's prayer list who are sick, traveling, grieving, or simply desiring the prayers of the church family. Writing cards to those members to encourage them can be an area of service for those with mental illnesses. It may even serve as an encouragement to those who are doing the writing and sending. Helping someone else to feel better can have the same effect on the one doing the assisting.

Meal preparation for the sick-and-shut-in is something that can be done from the comfort of one's home. And the delivery of meals does not involve contact with large crowds of people. It is another area of service. And some congregations sew bears for sick children in the hospital or provide snacks for family members in waiting areas. Learning and participating in the creation of stuffed animals that will bring joy to so many kids can be uplifting—even delivering them. And families are always extremely appreciative. The Christian who has a mental illness can benefit from serving in that capacity.

It is also recommended that Christians who struggle with mental health conditions like anxiety and depression assist in the church's food pantry. It is a fairly secluded task that can be done with minimal contact and interaction with others. Organizing food items and packing bags or boxes of food for those in need will help the giver and receiver, and it satisfies the command to feed those who are hungry (Matthew 25:37-40).

When the congregation I worship with hosted a community-wide event, I wanted to participate, but I knew that lots of people would be there and that would not sit well with my anxieties and paranoid thoughts. A dear sister, who knew of my struggles, recommended that I work in the kitchen. That way, I would not be bogged down with the crowd but could still serve (quite literally, actually). It worked out that I was in the kitchen helping, and I was able to contribute to the work without having a panic attack.

Although a Christian who is experiencing the effects of a mental illness may be limited in their daily activities and functioning, there are still many opportunities for them to serve. We just have to be aware of those limitations that we or others may have and know which direction to point them—like the sister did for me.

Having a mental illness is not a death sentence. It does not mean that you can no longer serve the Lord and other people. It means that you have to be careful and conscientious of the choices available to you, so you can still be the servant that Jesus has called us all to be (Matthew 23:11).

Questions for Reflection

1. Read Acts 9:36-40. How did Dorcas serve others, and how could what she did work for someone who has a mental illness?

2. List some other ways someone who is struggling with anxieties and phobias can serve in the work of the church.

3. Read Matthew 23:10-12. What did Jesus say about the one who is greatest?

4. A mental illness could be considered a thorn in the flesh. Who in the Bible had a thorn in the flesh but continued to serve the Lord? See 2 Corinthians 1:1; 12:7-8.

5. Read Mark 10:45. What were some ways that Jesus served others? Note your Scripture references.

CONCLUSION

Remember how I told you I fled the state – running from the law? Well, technically I was not running from the law – just the sheriff who was going to take me away or two men in white coats. I was gone from my hometown for nearly two years and angry at my family the entire time for trying to have me committed. I had made it a point to not talk to them ever again. But the Lord had a different plan in mind.

He did not want me to hold on to all that bitterness, anger, and resentment. Although anger is a natural emotion, it was not healthy for me to hold on to it for long. And it was not Christ-like to be unforgiving. Jesus reminds us: *"But if you do not forgive, neither will your Father in heaven forgive your trespasses"* (Mark 11:26). See, if I wanted to be forgiven by God of my wrongs, then I had to forgive others. I had to forgive my family for what they had done.

And I did. They simply did not know much or anything about mental illness. They did not know how to approach me about it. And they did not know how much their actions would hurt me. Mental health was never something we had talked about as a family – not growing up or into adulthood. Neither was it ever discussed in the church. It was sort of taboo. But it does not have to continue to be that way. Creating an open dialogue around mental health conditions like anxiety, depression, schizophrenia, and other mental illnesses can strengthen our families, our churches, and our communities.

If we do not proactively educate ourselves and work to prepare ourselves for mental illness, then we or our loved ones may suffer lasting negative effects. For me, it was the temporary separation from my family and primary support system. Unfortunately for others, it is more permanent with consequences like death-by-suicide. But we can prevent suicide from happening by having a safety plan in place and making a commitment to ourselves to live, no matter how difficult life gets.

Fast forward five years later. I am now back in my home state where my family resides. We are all on speaking terms and often spend time together. Our relationships have been mended through the power of forgiveness. Jesus forgave me of all of my wrongs when he died on the cruel cross of Calvary. So, I have to extend that forgiveness to others. It is quite freeing, actually. Being angry and hurt takes up a lot of energy – energy that I did not have to spare from dealing with my mental illness.

Being sick mentally can drain a woman of her vitality. In addition to being anxious, being depressed, being fearful, and being uncomfortable in her own environment, she has to be concerned with the daily cares of living, like cooking, cleaning, eating, and other activities. It is no wonder why many people who are mentally ill end up homeless or disproportionately incarcerated.

I know that dealing with my agoraphobia and anxiety disorders would have rendered me homeless many times. I could not leave my house! And jobs that I found that were work-from-home wanted me to be on screen, and I was already paranoid about cameras. So, I could not hold down a job for long either. If it was not for God surrounding me with loving and supportive people who cared about me, I do not know where I would be. But thanks be to God for His kindness towards me!

I now am able to work in an office around other people, although with the pandemic, I have mostly been working from home. I live on my own without the constant dread and fear of others breaking into my home. There are no doors boarded up with wood from the inside to keep people from entering without my consent. And I have made considerable progress as it relates to my paranoia and schizophrenia. This is mostly due to my compliance with my medication regimen. Medication, therapy, and other techniques of healing have greatly reduced my symptoms and the resulting actions that follow.

You can live a successful and fulfilling life with a mental illness. Just because you may be depressed or suicidal now does not mean that you will be the next month, or the next week – the next day, even. Sometimes, it simply takes time to get better. It will not always happen overnight. You just have to be patient with the process.

We have discussed several aspects of the process in moving towards healing and wholeness from a mental illness. We talked about prayer as an avenue to communicate with God your needs and your heart's desires. Hannah provides a great example for us. One can also partake in exercise, relaxation, and meditating on God's Word. And taking one's medication and participating in counseling sessions are also key in gaining control over one's mental health conditions.

My prayer to God for you is that you will be proactive rather than reactive when it comes to mental health. Hopefully this book will spur you to discuss mental illness more openly with your loved ones and other sisters and brothers in Christ. You may be surprised to find out who actually struggles with a mental health condition.

Many people call on the prayers of the church for their physical ailments, but we rarely hear of prayer requests for someone's depression, anxiety, or other mental illness. Hopefully, we can change that. Being sick mentally is akin to being sick physically.

We have dived into the Scriptures and seen that mental illnesses and the symptoms that accompany them are not so uncommon, as one might think. We must take great care of ourselves when we are sick mentally, just as we would if we had a physical ailment. That includes following the doctor's orders, taking medication, and changing our thinking so that our actions will follow.

It worked for me and is still working for me. I know that it can and will work for others, too. The future looks bright, and I can hardly wait to see what God has in store for me next.

I just want you to know that there is hope. There is hope for a better and brighter day ahead for you and your loved one. Everything will not always be so bleak, even if it feels that way. Anxiety, depression, paranoia, or suicidal thoughts do not have to get the best of you. Being diagnosed with a mental illness is not an automatic death sentence. It does not mean you are less God-fearing or to any degree worse than the next person. You can come out on the other side of it closer to the Lord – better and happier.

May God bless you with wellness and wholeness is my prayer.

www.ingramcontent.com/pod-product-compliance
Lightning Source LLC
LaVergne TN
LVHW010838120826
845149LV00017B/3305

* 9 7 9 8 9 9 5 4 9 6 1 0 6 *